# Heavy Air

Roadwork

Boxing Gyms

Uk/Thailand/Cambodia

Introduction/Eamonn McCabe.

This edition first published in 2018.
www.charliedontsurf.org.uk

Copyright Nigel Watmough 2018.
Copyright Eamonn McCabe 2018.
Copyright for individual texts rests with the authors.

Design by Mark Holiday.

ISBN:978-0-9935517-1-0
Heavy Air-Roadwork-East London/BKK/Cambodia.

## Credits

The majority of these images were taken at Lennox Lewis College, Clapton E5 between 2000-2004 including various boxers from the GB Olympic team (2000), Carl Froch, Rob McCracken and Mick Hennessy's team. Thanks to all concerned.

Thanks too to Colin Dunne and Terry Toole. Also featured are bouts at York Hall, Bethnal Green (E2) and training gyms in South Yorkshire, including Terry Petersen gym, Tadcaster Arms, Armthorpe.

Research into Thai boxing took me to Jitty's gym, down an alley off the Khao San Road and to bouts at Ratchadamnoen and Lumpini stadiums to cover traditional Muay Thai boxing and betting madness.

Also, thanks to Eh Phutong, Khmer boxing champ, for his hospitality and access to his training camp and to Master Sean Kim San, Boxcator federation, traditional Khmer Martial Arts, and to Antonio Graceffo for the contact.

Last, but not least, respect to Mr Pen my bikeman/fixer for his help. A chance meeting on St. # 19 opened up an alternative universe.

South Yorkshire, 1984. You couldn't get arrested unless you were on the picket line. I was looking for work, two years on the rock and roll, no prospects, just wearing out shoe leather. Finally I took a job in Sheffield, contacting and printing 10,000 plate glass negatives for Forgemasters documenting the steel industry from the 1930's to the 1950's which became a travelling exhibition sponsored by Pirelli.

When the contract ended I took the train to London working for a succession of B/W photo labs (Robin Bell/Roy Snell) and assisting on car shoots.

Meanwhile, working as an assistant at Christie's South Kensington, I put together a portfolio of portraits and got work from magazines like Ikon and 442 while shooting reportage in boxing gyms in East London.

A chance meeting with Kendo Nagasaki led to a portrait session (masked) in King's Cross and covering wrestling bouts at Fairfield Hall, Croydon.

Moving from sports entertainment to the real deal, I photographed Muay Thai in BKK and Khmer boxing at gyms and stadiums in Phnom Penh, along with a sequence of reportage on boxing at Lennox Lewis gym, York Hall, Wembley Conference Centre, and gyms in South Yorkshire.

Thanks to all trainers and fighters concerned.

Locations

The images in this book started with a series of photos taken late October 1999 at Terry Petersen gym in the basement of the Tadcaster Arms, Armthorpe, Doncaster and then at bouts at York Hall, Bethnal Green and Wembley Conference Centre. (As we entered York Hall, Terry handed me a bucket and sponge and I became a corner man for the night-best seat in the house). Subsequently, I covered Muay Thai at Jitty's gym, BKK and Lumpini Stadium as well as training at Lennox Lewis gym, Clapton, E5 and Rob McCracken with Carl Froch and various Olympic GB Team boxers who had turned professional.

Amateur gyms and boxers were featured in South Yorkshire-Armthorpe, Highfields, Bolton-on-Dearne and pro fights at Barnsley Metrodome and Nottingham Arena.

Thai Boxing was at Lumpini and Ratchadamnoen Stadiums, while in Phnom Penh I worked at various locations including Olympic Stadium and Eh Phuthong gym. I would like to thank all boxers, trainers, managers, agencies and promoters who gave me time and access to get these shots.

The one time I was denied access ringside at the classic "throwback fight"- Colin Dunne v Billy Schwer, Wembley, 14/10/2000, I got a cracking shot of Colin, totally in the zone, leaving for the ring. "Sometimes nothing can be a real cool hand."

"Railroad yard San Jose."

In Back of the Real. Ginsberg 1954.


"Sometimes, nothing can be a real cool hand."

Cool Hand Luke. 1967.

Special thanks to

**Eamonn McCabe**

for advice and insight, encouragement
and responding at short notice to yet another tight deadline.
www.eamonnmccabe.co.uk

"Don't count the days, make the days count."-Ali.

Boxing

Eamonn McCabe

I have always enjoyed photographing loners. I love photographing painters, poets and writers. I am intrigued by their private spaces and it always feels a privilege to be allowed in, often on my own.

But the loneliest people I have ever photographed are boxers.

Once you get in that ring there is no turning back and there is nobody to help you; you are truly alone. Even in a noisy, sweaty gym while training for a fight you are on your own. You cannot take a rest as a footballer would while the ball is up the field.

If you stop, you get hit and you get hurt.

Some of my best photographs for The Observer were taken way back in the 'seventies and 'eighties in boxing gyms around the world along with my great friend Hugh McIlvanney, the doyen of sports writers. I wanted to show the readers something they would never see on TV.

Loners are driven - that's why I like them so much. And I want to learn from them, what makes them motivated on their own, what keeps them going? I have always hoped that drive would rub off on me.

I remember in 1985 I went to the border between Eire and Northern Ireland to watch the great Barry McGuigan train for a world title fight in London against Eusebio Pedroza, which he won. He pummelled away for two hours above a pub in front of his manager Barney Eastwood and when he was happy with his work he got dressed and went down to the bar for a drink and an interview with Hugh.

After the chat Eastwood left with Hugh to go back to Belfast and McGuigan made me swear not to tell Barney, but he went back upstairs and did another two hours. No wonder he was world champion.

Another boxer who made great photographs for me was Johnny Owen. He was too tall and too thin to be a boxer - in fact so thin that he was nicknamed The Merthyr Matchstick - but he made it to Los Angeles in 1980 for a world title fight, where unfortunately he died soon after the contest with the Mexican Lupe Pintor.

Again Hugh and I were working above a pub in Merthyr Tydfil in Wales and Johnny went through his repertoire of moves and punches which made great pictures. When he finished he had a shower and came out naked and got on some old-fashioned scales. What a picture I thought, as I excitedly loaded my Leica M2 camera a tricky camera to load at the best of times, but especially when you can see a great photograph and are fumbling with excitement.

I shot a few frames and my heart was pumping; this will look great in the paper, I thought. I went downstairs to have a drink with everyone and started to rewind my film into the camera. Then it happened - the worst feeling in the world - after one turn the film had fully loaded back into the cassette. I took some of the best photographs I have ever seen, but they were sadly not recorded on film.

I knew I had nothing and that the moment had gone, I couldn't ask him to do it again as it would never have looked right. That was the longest journey back to London I can ever remember. And the worst thing was I could never tell anybody, until now.

Over the years I was lucky to photograph some of the greats; Marvin Hagler, Roberto Duran and Larry Holmes, but the biggest star was Mike Tyson. I had left the Observer in 1986 to become picture editor of Sportsweek Magazine, which Robert Maxwell had started up as a British version of Sports Illustrated. I was in heaven choosing the best sports pictures from around the world.

It only lasted six months and fortunately the Observer welcomed me back with open arms. The first assignment I was to do for them on my return was Mike Tyson training in a gym in Vegas and which was hugely publicised as my return to the paper.

I flew over having set it all up with his management, got to the gym in boiling white sunlight and waited for him to appear. He duly arrived in dark glasses, and huge floppy hat to protect him from the heat and grunted as he went by to disappear into the gym.

I knocked nervously a little later and his manager said: "Eamonn, Mike doesn't want to do it today, could you come back tomorrow?" I was on a tight deadline and had to leave that night to get back to London in time for Sunday's paper. After much pleading they relented. I was going to be able to photograph the most famous boxer on the planet at that time, as he left the gym and walked to the limo waiting in the shade a few feet away.

I waited an hour in the hottest sun I can ever remember, practising focusing every yard of that car park. It was going to be alright I kept telling myself. And then he appeared, hat pulled down over his face, never stopped once and just fell into the limo.

I spent the whole of the red-eye flight back to London convincing myself that I could see him, and that it would be okay. I processed the film and had a great photograph........ of a hat!

The Observer published it after all the hullabaloo of the previous week about my return, but you could barely make out who it was.

Looking at Nigel Watmough's photographs in this great new book I can again smell the sweat and the liniment and the strongest smell of all - fear.

Last year I made a film for BBC4 on the history of photography in Britain and one of the places I wanted to go back to was York Hall in Bethnal Green in the east end of London where it all started for me, working on local papers.

After forty years nothing has changed; the lights, the colour, the noise, the swearing and the boxing were all still as great. I photographed several bouts where the boxers put everything into it.

Such an honest, hard, lonely craft and after all this time I even got a few photographs sharp.

Eamonn McCabe was sports photographer of the year a record four times.

York Hall, Bethnal Green, E2.
Russian boxer 16/9/2000.

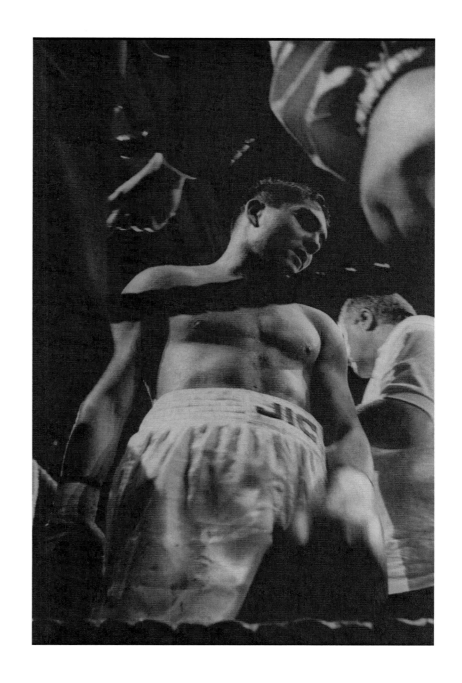

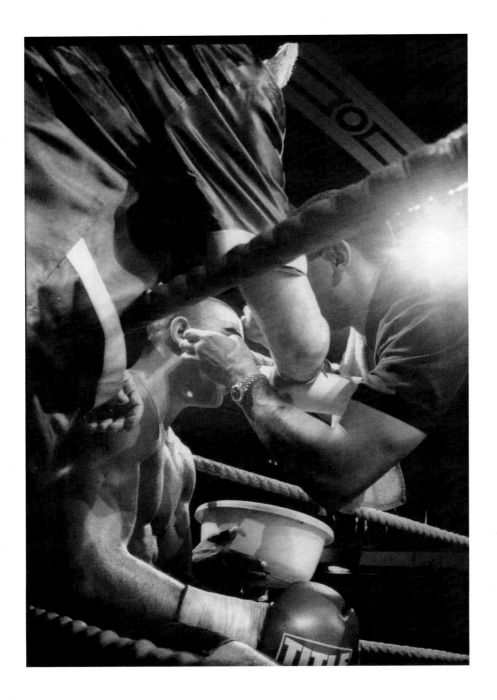

Corner, York Hall
16/9/2000

Corner, York Hall.
16/9/2000

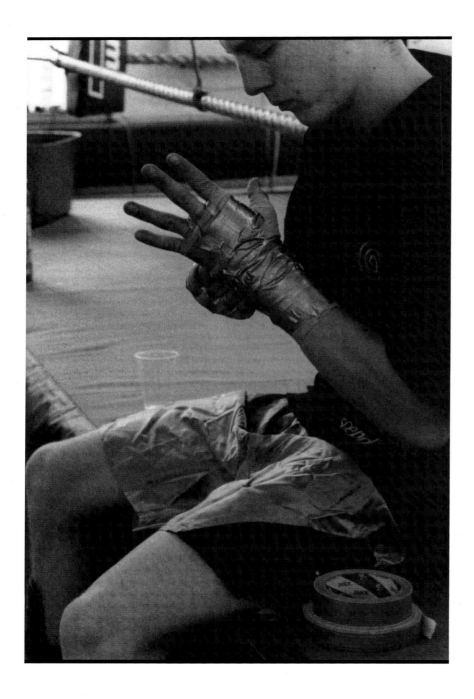

Lee/wraps/Lennox Lewis gym, E3.
8/9/2000

Andrew/tapes/Lennox Lewis gym.
8/9/2000

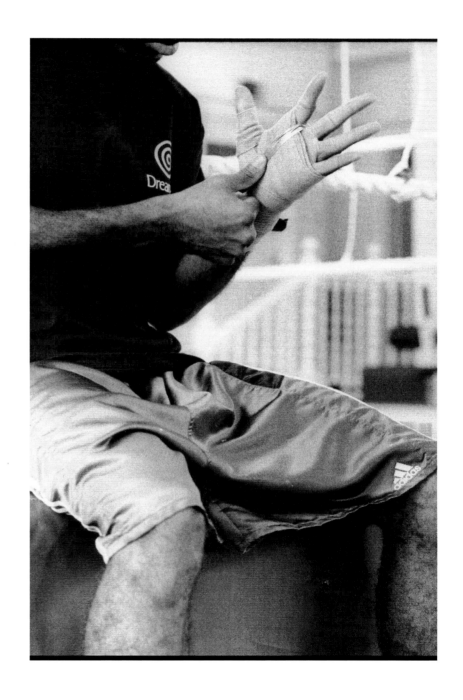

Lee Meager/Dreamcast.
8/9/2000

Tapes/Lennox Lewis gym, E3.
5/3/2004

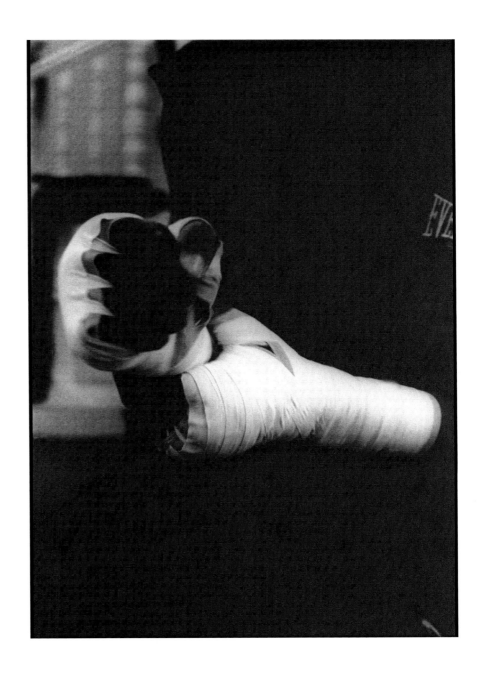

Lee/sparring/Lennox Lewis gym E3.
8/9/2000

David Walker and Rob McCracken, E3.
23/1/2002

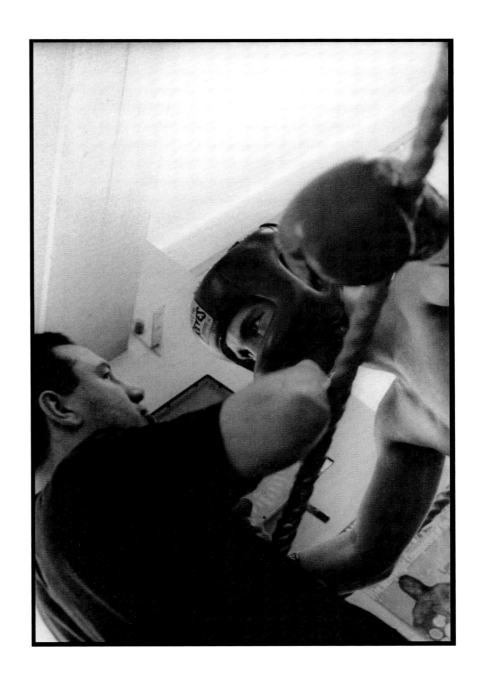

David Walker/Lennox Lewis gym, E3.
23/1/2002

David Walker, sparring. E3.
23/1/2002

David Walker, wraps, E3.
23/1/2002

Boxer (foreground) + Carl Froch, Lennox Lewis gym, E3.
23/1/2002

Boxer, Lennox Lewis gym, E3.
23/1/2002

Colin Dunne and Terry Toole, Lennox Lewis gym, E3.
13/9/2000

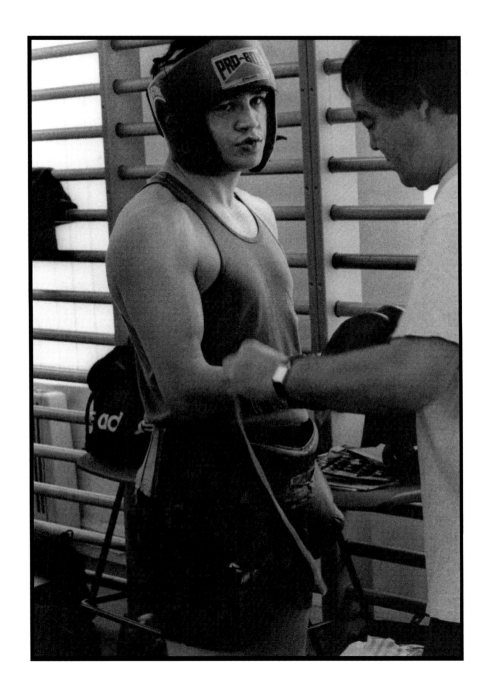

Colin Dunne leaving dressing room for ring (Billy Schwer fight/WBU title fight) Wembley Conference Centre. 14/10/2000

Carl Froch and Lee Meager, corner.
23/1/2002

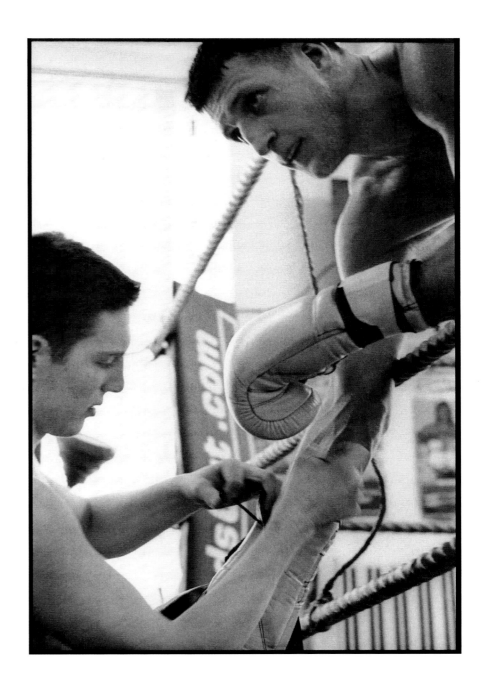

Boxers, Lennox Lewis gym.
23/1/2002

Carl Froch and Rob McCracken, Nottingham Arena.
12/3/2004

Corner, Barnsley Metrodome.
28/3/2008

Corner, Barnsley Metrodome.
28/3/2008

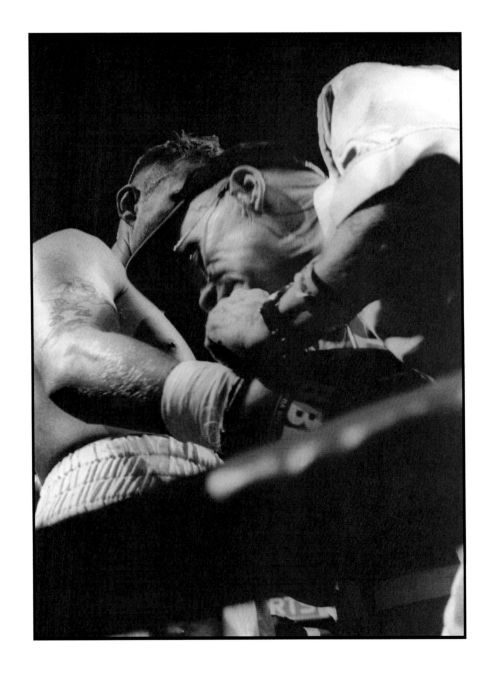

Corner, Barnsley Metrodome.
28/3/2008

Corner, Barnsley Metrodome.
28/3/2008

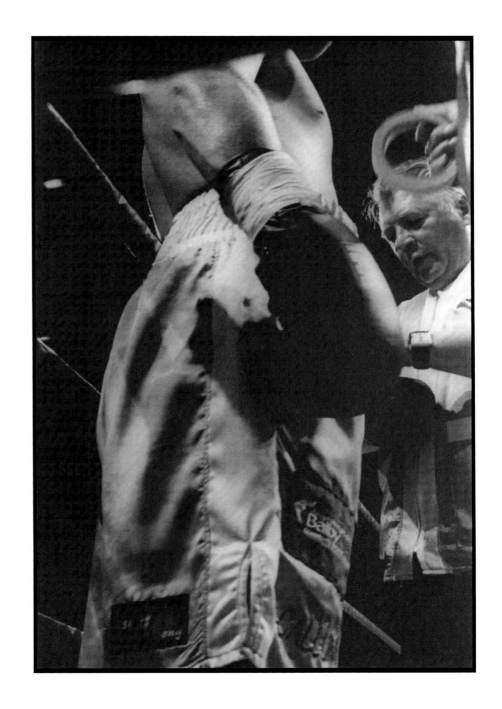

Cornerman, Barnsley Metrodome.
28/3/2008

Carl Froch at Lennox Lewis gym, E3.
23/1/2002

Medicine ball workout, Highfields gym.

21/11/2006

Speedball workout, Bolton-on-Dearne, South Yorkshire.
22/3/2006

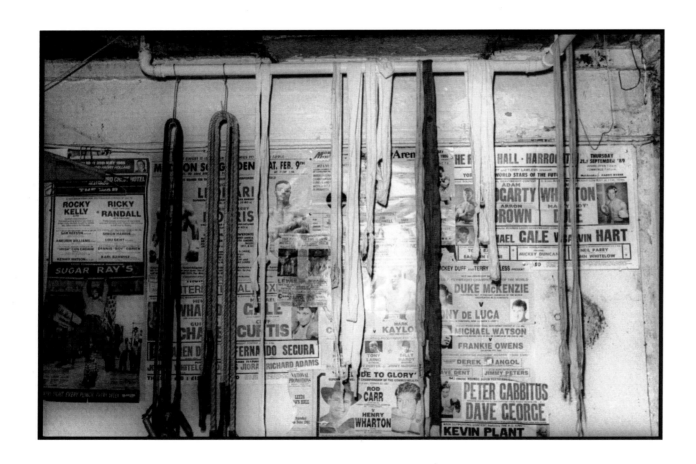

Wraps and speedropes,
Terry Petersen Gym
Armthorpe 1999.

Terry Petersen gym,
Tadcaster Arms,
Armthorpe.
27/10/1999

# Boxing gyms
# Thailand & Cambodia

Posed shot, champ, Lumpini.
2003

Corner, Lumpini, BKK.
2/11/2004

Young Thai boxer entering ring.

5/11/2004

Corner, Lumpini.

2/11/2004

Corner, Lumpini.

2/11/2004

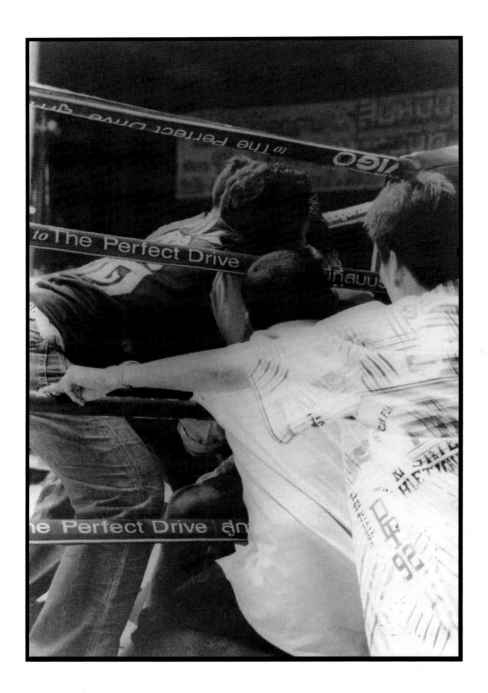

Corner, Lumpini.
2/11/2004

KHMER boxer, Phnom Penh.
Nov 2002

Corner, Khmer boxing, Phnom Penh.
23/8/2003

Olympic gym, Phnom Penh.

Nov 2002

Posed shot, Post-fight,
Lumpini.
28/1/2000

Olympic gym,
Phnom Penh.
Nov 2002

Jitty's gym, BKK.

24/1/2000

Tattoo, Olympic gym.
May 2011

Tattoo, Eh Phutong gym, Phnom Penh.
May 2011

Corner, Lumpini,
BKK.
2/11/2004

Corner, Lumpini, BKK.
2/11/2004

Boxcator gym, Phnom Penh.
9/12/2007

Colin Dunne, Brentwood Centre.
(Colin' Dynamo' Dunne v Esteban Morales
21/9/2002).

There isn't enough space to acknowledge all the people who have been instrumental in the concept, excecution of this book "Heavy Air". I will try to list them individually, apologies for any omissions.

Special thanks to: My Parents, Betty and Hedley Watmough for love and support.

Juice and Kerry.

Marion Slater.

Boxers, trainers, managers at training camps and gyms (UK, BKK, Phnom Penh.) as detailed in the intro-Respect.

Sensei P.J.L. Davies/ Yawara Ryu (Bob, Pete, Nicky and team).

Sensei Bill Rankin/ Gunji Koizumi.

Robin Bell/ Hugo Platt/ Roy Snell-introduction to the dark arts.

Mark Holiday Design Guru.

X-Man/ AJ. /Tony Nourmand.

Dr K Brennan-access, ringside, Barnsley Metrodome, 2008.

Martin Thompson Studios, Caledonian Road, N1 9DX/the A-Team.

Nuzz.

Rangsophen/driver, fixer, main man.

Fletch, Cheryl and Russell.

JB and Bua (Guinness, BKK).

Reedy and Janey.

Trout and the guys in front bar, Little Plough.

"I've been in the right place
But it must have been the wrong time."
Dr John.


If you see it in the viewfinder, you missed the shot-that's the wisdom of the guys ringside.
It's true in boxing and, I imagine, sports photography in general.

The sound of one hand snapping.

Eamonn McCabe - www.eamonnmccabe.co.uk

Mark Holiday - www.markholiday.co.uk   www.gullwickstravels.com

Nigel Watmough (Reportage) - www.charliedontsurf.org.uk


Clarke Carlisle Foundation for Dual Diagnosis.

e: ccdd@btinternet.com


not a red card campaign. :www.legalandgeneral.com/notaredcard.